EMMANUEL JOSEPH

Philanthropy Unbound, How the Wealthy Rewrite the Rules of Giving

Copyright © 2025 by Emmanuel Joseph

All rights reserved. No part of this publication may be reproduced, stored or transmitted in any form or by any means, electronic, mechanical, photocopying, recording, scanning, or otherwise without written permission from the publisher. It is illegal to copy this book, post it to a website, or distribute it by any other means without permission.

First edition

This book was professionally typeset on Reedsy.
Find out more at reedsy.com

Contents

1. Chapter 1: The Dawn of Modern Philanthropy — 1
2. Chapter 2: The Rise of the Tech Titans — 3
3. Chapter 3: The Impact of Globalization on Philanthropy — 5
4. Chapter 4: Innovative Funding Models — 7
5. Chapter 5: The Power of Collaboration — 9
6. Chapter 6: The Role of Technology in Philanthropy — 11
7. Chapter 7: The Intersection of Philanthropy and Social... — 13
8. Chapter 8: The Influence of Corporate Philanthropy — 15
9. Chapter 9: The Role of Family Foundations — 17
10. Chapter 10: The Ethics of Philanthropy — 19
11. Chapter 11: The Role of Philanthropy in Education — 21
12. Chapter 12: The Role of Philanthropy in Healthcare — 23
13. Chapter 13: Philanthropy and the Arts — 25
14. Chapter 14: The Future of Philanthropy — 27
15. Chapter 15: The Intersection of Philanthropy and Politics — 29
16. Chapter 16: Philanthropy in Times of Crisis — 31
17. Chapter 17: The Legacy of Philanthropy — 33

1

Chapter 1: The Dawn of Modern Philanthropy

In the early 20th century, a new era of philanthropy began to take shape. Wealthy individuals like Andrew Carnegie and John D. Rockefeller set the stage for modern philanthropy by establishing large foundations aimed at addressing societal issues. Their approach to giving was strategic and focused on creating long-term impact. Unlike the charity of the past, which often provided temporary relief, these philanthropists sought to address the root causes of problems and create lasting change.

Carnegie, for instance, believed in the "Gospel of Wealth," a philosophy that advocated for the wealthy to use their resources for the betterment of society. He established libraries, schools, and universities, believing that education was the key to social progress. Similarly, Rockefeller's philanthropy focused on public health, education, and scientific research. He funded the establishment of the Rockefeller Institute for Medical Research and the General Education Board, which aimed to improve education in the United States.

This new approach to philanthropy was not without its critics. Some argued that the immense power and influence wielded by these wealthy individuals could lead to a concentration of power and undermine democratic processes. Critics also pointed out that the wealth accumulated by these philanthropists was often the result of exploitative business practices. Nevertheless, their contributions laid the foundation for modern philanthropy and set a precedent for future generations of wealthy individuals.

As the 20th century progressed, the landscape of philanthropy continued to evolve. The rise of new industries and the accumulation of wealth by tech entrepreneurs in the late 20th and early 21st centuries brought a new wave of philanthropic efforts. These modern philanthropists, such as Bill Gates and Warren Buffett, followed in the footsteps of Carnegie and Rockefeller, but also introduced new approaches and priorities in their giving.

2

Chapter 2: The Rise of the Tech Titans

The late 20th and early 21st centuries saw the rise of a new breed of philanthropists – tech entrepreneurs who amassed vast fortunes through their innovative companies. Figures like Bill Gates, Warren Buffett, and Mark Zuckerberg emerged as prominent philanthropists, leveraging their wealth to tackle global challenges. These tech titans brought a unique approach to philanthropy, characterized by a focus on data-driven solutions, innovative funding models, and a global perspective.

Bill Gates, co-founder of Microsoft, and his wife Melinda established the Bill and Melinda Gates Foundation in 2000. The foundation's mission is to enhance healthcare, reduce extreme poverty, and expand educational opportunities worldwide. Gates' approach to philanthropy is heavily influenced by his background in technology and data analysis. The foundation invests in research and development, emphasizing the importance of evidence-based interventions and scalable solutions. Through initiatives such as the Global Health Program and the Global Development Program, the Gates Foundation has made significant strides in combating diseases like malaria, tuberculosis, and HIV/AIDS.

Warren Buffett, one of the most successful investors of all time, has also made substantial contributions to philanthropy. In 2006, he announced his decision to donate the majority of his fortune to the Gates Foundation and other charitable organizations. Buffett's approach to philanthropy is pragmatic and rooted in his belief that the wealthy have a moral obligation to give back to society. His commitment to philanthropy has inspired other billionaires to pledge their fortunes through initiatives like The Giving Pledge, which he co-founded with Bill Gates.

Mark Zuckerberg, the co-founder of Facebook, represents a younger generation of tech philanthropists. In 2015, Zuckerberg and his wife Priscilla Chan pledged to donate 99% of their Facebook shares to charitable causes through the Chan Zuckerberg Initiative (CZI). The CZI focuses on areas such as education, healthcare, and scientific research, aiming to create a more inclusive and equitable future. Zuckerberg's philanthropic vision is driven by a belief in the power of technology and innovation to address complex social issues.

These tech philanthropists have not only reshaped the landscape of giving but have also sparked a broader conversation about the role of wealth and power in society. Their influence extends beyond their financial contributions, as they advocate for systemic change and challenge traditional models of philanthropy.

3

Chapter 3: The Impact of Globalization on Philanthropy

Globalization has had a profound impact on philanthropy, expanding the scope and reach of charitable efforts. In an interconnected world, philanthropists can address issues that transcend national borders, such as climate change, global health, and education. This global perspective has led to the emergence of international foundations and cross-border collaborations aimed at tackling some of the world's most pressing challenges.

One of the key trends in global philanthropy is the rise of international foundations. These organizations, often funded by wealthy individuals and families, operate on a global scale and focus on issues that affect multiple countries. The Ford Foundation, for example, has a long history of supporting international development and human rights initiatives. Founded in 1936, the foundation has funded projects in over 60 countries, addressing issues such as poverty, gender equality, and social justice.

Another example is the Open Society Foundations, established by billionaire financier George Soros. The network of foundations and partners works to promote democracy, human rights, and social reform in over 120 countries. Soros' approach to philanthropy emphasizes the importance of open societies and the rule of law, with a focus on supporting grassroots organizations and civil society.

Globalization has also facilitated cross-border collaborations between philanthropic organizations, governments, and international agencies. These partnerships leverage the resources and expertise of multiple stakeholders to address complex global issues. For instance, the Global Fund to Fight AIDS, Tuberculosis, and Malaria is a public-private partnership that mobilizes resources to combat these diseases in low- and middle-income countries. The fund has saved millions of lives by providing access to treatment, prevention, and care services.

The impact of globalization on philanthropy is not without its challenges. Critics argue that the influence of wealthy donors and international foundations can undermine local priorities and perpetuate power imbalances. Additionally, the lack of transparency and accountability in some philanthropic efforts has raised concerns about the effectiveness and legitimacy of global giving. Despite these challenges, the globalization of philanthropy has the potential to drive significant progress in addressing global challenges and promoting social change.

4

Chapter 4: Innovative Funding Models

The landscape of philanthropy has been transformed by the emergence of innovative funding models that leverage the power of markets and private capital. These new approaches to giving aim to create sustainable impact by blending financial returns with social and environmental goals. Impact investing, social entrepreneurship, and venture philanthropy are some of the key funding models that have gained prominence in recent years.

Impact investing is an investment strategy that seeks to generate both financial returns and positive social or environmental outcomes. Unlike traditional philanthropy, which relies on grants and donations, impact investing mobilizes private capital to support businesses and organizations that address social and environmental challenges. Investors in this space seek to align their financial goals with their values, supporting projects that have the potential to create meaningful change. Examples of impact investments include renewable energy projects, affordable housing, and sustainable agriculture.

Social entrepreneurship is another innovative approach to philanthropy that combines business principles with a social mission. Social entrepreneurs identify and address societal problems through innovative, market-based solutions. These enterprises often operate as for-profit businesses, with the revenue generated used to fund their social initiatives. One well-known example is TOMS Shoes, a company that donates a pair of shoes to a child in need for every pair sold. Social entrepreneurship has gained traction as a way to create scalable and sustainable impact, leveraging the efficiency and innovation of the private sector.

Venture philanthropy is a funding model that applies the principles of venture capital to philanthropy. This approach involves providing funding, strategic support, and capacity-building to nonprofit organizations and social enterprises. Venture philanthropists take an active role in the organizations they support, working closely with them to achieve their goals and drive social change. The model emphasizes long-term partnerships, measurable outcomes, and the use of data to inform decision-making. The Silicon Valley Social Venture Fund (SV2) is an example of an organization that follows this approach, supporting innovative solutions to social and environmental challenges.

These innovative funding models represent a shift in the way philanthropy is practiced, moving away from traditional grant-making to more strategic and outcome-focused approaches. By leveraging private capital, business principles, and market-based solutions, these models have the potential to drive significant social and environmental impact.

5

Chapter 5: The Power of Collaboration

In the realm of modern philanthropy, collaboration has become a key driver of impact. Wealthy individuals, foundations, and corporations are increasingly working together to pool resources, share knowledge, and amplify their efforts. Collaborative initiatives allow philanthropists to address complex social issues more effectively by leveraging the strengths and expertise of multiple stakeholders.

One notable example of collaboration in philanthropy is the Partnership for a Healthier America (PHA). Founded in 2010, PHA brings together government, business, and philanthropic leaders to combat childhood obesity and promote healthier lifestyles. The partnership works with food and beverage companies, retailers, and community organizations to make healthier options more accessible and affordable. By aligning the efforts of diverse stakeholders, PHA has been able to drive significant progress in improving public health.

Another example is the ClimateWorks Foundation, which collaborates with a network of partners to address climate change. The foundation funds and coordinates efforts to reduce greenhouse gas emissions and promote sustainable energy solutions. Through partnerships with other foundations, NGOs, and government agencies, ClimateWorks is able to maximize its impact and drive systemic change in the fight against climate change.

Collaborative initiatives are not limited to formal partnerships. Informal networks and alliances also play a crucial role in modern philanthropy. For instance, the Skoll World Forum on Social Entrepreneurship is an annual gathering that brings together philanthropists, social entrepreneurs, and thought leaders to share ideas and collaborate on innovative solutions to global challenges. These types of events foster connections and facilitate the exchange of knowledge and best practices, ultimately enhancing the effectiveness of philanthropic efforts.

The power of collaboration extends beyond the immediate impact of philanthropic projects. By working together, philanthropists can influence public policy, drive systemic change, and create a broader movement for social good. Collaborative efforts help to amplify the voices of marginalized communities, promote equity, and address the root causes of social issues.

6

Chapter 6: The Role of Technology in Philanthropy

Technology has revolutionized the way philanthropy is practiced, enabling new forms of giving and enhancing the impact of charitable efforts. From online fundraising platforms to data analytics, technology has transformed the landscape of philanthropy and opened up new possibilities for addressing social challenges.

One of the most significant technological advancements in philanthropy is the rise of online fundraising platforms. Websites like GoFundMe, Kickstarter, and GlobalGiving have democratized philanthropy by allowing individuals and small organizations to raise funds for their causes. These platforms provide a space for donors to connect with projects they are passionate about and contribute to initiatives that might not have access to traditional funding sources. Crowdfunding campaigns have supported a wide range of causes, from medical expenses and disaster relief to educational programs and social enterprises.

Data analytics and artificial intelligence (AI) are also playing a crucial role in modern philanthropy. By harnessing the power of data, philanthropists can make more informed decisions and allocate resources more effectively. For example, data analytics can help identify the most pressing needs in a community, assess the impact of charitable programs, and track progress towards goals. AI-powered tools can also be used to analyze large datasets, uncover patterns, and predict outcomes, enabling philanthropists to design more targeted and impactful interventions.

Technology has also facilitated greater transparency and accountability in philanthropy. Digital platforms and tools allow donors to track how their contributions are being used and measure the impact of their giving. Websites like GuideStar and Charity Navigator provide information on the financial health, accountability, and transparency of nonprofit organizations, helping donors make more informed decisions about where to allocate their funds.

Moreover, technology has enabled new forms of collaboration and knowledge-sharing among philanthropists. Online networks and platforms, such as the Philanthropy Exchange and the Center for Effective Philanthropy, provide spaces for philanthropists to connect, share insights, and collaborate on initiatives. These digital communities foster innovation and enhance the collective impact of philanthropic efforts.

7

Chapter 7: The Intersection of Philanthropy and Social Justice

In recent years, there has been a growing recognition of the need to address social justice issues within the realm of philanthropy. Wealthy individuals and foundations are increasingly focusing on initiatives that promote equity, inclusion, and systemic change. This shift towards social justice philanthropy aims to address the root causes of inequality and create a more just and equitable society.

One key area of focus in social justice philanthropy is racial equity. The tragic events of the past decade, including incidents of police violence and racial injustice, have highlighted the urgent need to address systemic racism. Philanthropists are supporting initiatives that aim to dismantle structural barriers and promote racial equity. For example, the Ford Foundation launched the "America's Cultural Treasures" initiative, which provides funding to organizations led by and serving communities of color. This initiative aims to support and uplift historically marginalized voices and promote cultural diversity.

Gender equity is another important focus of social justice philanthropy. Wealthy donors are investing in programs that empower women and girls, address gender-based violence, and promote economic opportunities for women. The Bill and Melinda Gates Foundation, for instance, has made significant investments in initiatives that advance gender equality, such as promoting access to family planning, supporting women's leadership, and addressing gender-based violence.

Economic justice is also a critical aspect of social justice philanthropy. Philanthropists are working to address economic disparities and create opportunities for marginalized communities. Initiatives in this area include supporting job training and workforce development programs, promoting affordable housing, and advocating for fair wages and labor rights. The Open Society Foundations, for example, have funded projects that promote economic justice and support workers' rights.

Social justice philanthropy is not without its challenges. Addressing systemic inequality requires long-term commitment and collaboration with communities most affected by injustice. It also involves challenging existing power dynamics and ensuring that the voices of marginalized communities are centered in decision-making processes. Despite these challenges, the growing focus on social justice within philanthropy holds the promise of creating lasting and transformative change.

8

Chapter 8: The Influence of Corporate Philanthropy

Corporate philanthropy has become a significant force in the world of giving, as businesses increasingly recognize the importance of social responsibility. Many corporations now integrate philanthropy into their core business strategies, leveraging their resources, expertise, and influence to address societal challenges. Corporate philanthropy takes various forms, including direct donations, employee volunteer programs, and cause-related marketing campaigns.

One prominent example of corporate philanthropy is the work of Patagonia, an outdoor clothing and gear company. Patagonia has long been committed to environmental sustainability and social responsibility. The company donates 1% of its sales to environmental causes through its "1% for the Planet" initiative. Additionally, Patagonia supports grassroots environmental organizations and engages in activism to protect public lands and promote sustainable practices. The company's commitment to philanthropy is deeply embedded in its corporate culture and values.

Another example is Salesforce, a global leader in customer relationship management (CRM) software. Salesforce has pioneered the 1-1-1 model of corporate philanthropy, which dedicates 1% of the company's equity, 1% of its product, and 1% of employee time to charitable causes. Through the Salesforce Foundation, the company supports education, workforce development, and community service initiatives. The 1-1-1 model has inspired other companies to adopt similar approaches and prioritize social impact.

Corporate philanthropy is not limited to large multinational companies. Small and medium-sized enterprises (SMEs) also engage in philanthropic efforts, often focusing on local communities and causes. For example, local businesses may support schools, sports teams, and community events through donations and sponsorships. SMEs can also leverage their unique strengths and connections to drive positive change in their communities.

While corporate philanthropy has the potential to create significant social impact, it is not without its challenges. Critics argue that some companies use philanthropy as a form of "greenwashing" or "purpose-washing" to improve their public image without making meaningful changes to their business practices. Additionally, there are concerns about the concentration of power and influence in the hands of large corporations. To address these challenges, it is essential for companies to ensure transparency, accountability, and alignment between their philanthropic efforts and their overall business strategies.

9

Chapter 9: The Role of Family Foundations

Family foundations play a unique and influential role in the world of philanthropy. These foundations are often established by wealthy families to manage their charitable giving and create a legacy of impact. Family foundations are characterized by their long-term commitment to specific causes, personalized approaches to giving, and the involvement of multiple generations in philanthropic decision-making.

One well-known example of a family foundation is the Rockefeller Foundation, established by John D. Rockefeller in 1913. The foundation has a long history of supporting initiatives in public health, education, and scientific research. It has funded groundbreaking work in areas such as the development of vaccines, agricultural innovation, and urban resilience. The Rockefeller Foundation's enduring commitment to social impact has made it a model for other family foundations.

Another example is the Walton Family Foundation, created by the descendants of Walmart founder Sam Walton. The foundation focuses on education, environmental conservation, and economic development. It supports initiatives that aim to improve K-12 education, protect water resources, and promote economic mobility. The involvement of multiple generations of the Walton family in the foundation's work ensures that their philanthropic vision evolves over time while staying true to their core values.

Family foundations often take a highly personalized approach to philanthropy, reflecting the values and interests of the founding family. This allows for greater flexibility and responsiveness to emerging needs and opportunities. Family foundations can also leverage their networks and influence to drive systemic change and advocate for policy reforms.

However, family foundations face challenges as well. Ensuring effective governance and decision-making can be complex, especially as multiple generations and family members are involved. Additionally, there is a need for transparency and accountability to ensure that the foundation's resources are used effectively and ethically. Despite these challenges, family foundations have the potential to create lasting and meaningful impact through their philanthropic efforts.

10

Chapter 10: The Ethics of Philanthropy

The practice of philanthropy raises important ethical questions about power, accountability, and the role of wealth in society. As wealthy individuals and foundations wield significant influence through their charitable giving, it is essential to consider the ethical implications of their actions and decisions.

One key ethical concern in philanthropy is the potential for power imbalances. Wealthy donors often have the ability to shape public agendas, influence policy, and direct resources to specific causes. This concentration of power can undermine democratic processes and limit the voices of marginalized communities. To address this concern, it is important for philanthropists to engage with and listen to the communities they seek to support. Meaningful collaboration and participatory approaches can help ensure that philanthropic efforts are aligned with the needs and priorities of those most affected by social issues.

Another ethical consideration is the source of philanthropic wealth. Critics argue that some philanthropic donations are derived from exploitative or harmful business practices. For example, the accumulation of wealth through environmental degradation, labor exploitation, or tax avoidance raises questions about the legitimacy of philanthropic contributions. To address this issue, some philanthropists are adopting ethical investment practices and aligning their business operations with their philanthropic values. This approach ensures that their wealth is generated and used in ways that promote social and environmental sustainability.

Transparency and accountability are also critical ethical considerations in philanthropy. Donors and foundations must be transparent about their goals, strategies, and decision-making processes. This includes providing clear and accessible information about how funds are allocated and the impact of their initiatives. Accountability mechanisms, such as independent evaluations and audits, can help ensure that philanthropic efforts are effective and aligned with ethical standards.

Finally, the ethics of philanthropy also involves considering the long-term impact and sustainability of charitable efforts. Philanthropists must balance the desire for immediate results with the need for systemic change and lasting impact. This requires a thoughtful and strategic approach to giving, with a focus on addressing the root causes of social issues and promoting sustainable solutions.

11

Chapter 11: The Role of Philanthropy in Education

Education has long been a central focus of philanthropic efforts, as many wealthy individuals and foundations recognize the transformative power of education in improving lives and communities. Philanthropists have invested in various aspects of education, from early childhood development to higher education, and have supported initiatives aimed at increasing access, equity, and quality in education.

One prominent example of philanthropic support in education is the work of the Gates Foundation. The foundation has made significant investments in K-12 education, focusing on areas such as teacher effectiveness, standards and assessments, and personalized learning. Through initiatives like the College-Ready Education program, the Gates Foundation aims to ensure that all students graduate from high school prepared for college and career success. The foundation also supports efforts to increase access to postsecondary education through scholarships and financial aid programs.

Another example is the work of the Lumina Foundation, which is dedicated to increasing the number of Americans with high-quality postsecondary degrees and credentials. The foundation's goal is to ensure that 60% of Americans hold a postsecondary credential by 2025. To achieve this, Lumina supports initiatives that promote college affordability, improve student success, and align education with workforce needs. The foundation also advocates for policy reforms that enhance the accessibility and quality of higher education.

Philanthropic efforts in education are not limited to the United States. Globally, organizations like the Global Partnership for Education (GPE) work to improve education systems in developing countries. The GPE brings together governments, donors, international organizations, and civil society to provide funding and technical support to countries with the greatest educational needs. By focusing on equity, quality, and inclusion, the GPE aims to ensure that all children, regardless of their background, have access to a quality education.

While philanthropy has made significant contributions to education, it is not without its challenges. Critics argue that philanthropic efforts can sometimes undermine public education systems and promote privatization. Additionally, there are concerns about the accountability and transparency of philanthropic initiatives. To address these challenges, it is important for philanthropists to collaborate with educators, policymakers, and communities to ensure that their efforts are aligned with the needs and priorities of students and families.

12

Chapter 12: The Role of Philanthropy in Healthcare

Healthcare is another critical area where philanthropy has made a significant impact. Wealthy individuals and foundations have supported a wide range of healthcare initiatives, from funding medical research to improving access to healthcare services. Philanthropic efforts in healthcare aim to address pressing health challenges, reduce health disparities, and promote overall well-being.

One notable example of philanthropic support in healthcare is the work of the Wellcome Trust, one of the largest biomedical research charities in the world. The trust funds research in areas such as infectious diseases, neuroscience, and mental health. By supporting innovative research and fostering collaborations between scientists, the Wellcome Trust aims to improve our understanding of health and disease and develop new treatments and interventions.

Another example is the work of the Chan Zuckerberg Initiative (CZI), which has made significant investments in healthcare and scientific research. CZI's science program focuses on understanding the underlying causes of disease and developing new tools and technologies to accelerate scientific discovery. The initiative also supports efforts to improve access to quality healthcare and address social determinants of health, such as education, housing, and economic opportunity.

Philanthropic efforts in healthcare are not limited to research and innovation. Many foundations and organizations also work to improve access to healthcare services, particularly in underserved communities. For instance, the Robert Wood Johnson Foundation focuses on building a culture of health in the United States, with initiatives that address health equity, access to care, and the social determinants of health. The foundation supports programs that promote healthy behaviors, improve healthcare delivery, and create healthier communities.

Global health is another important focus of philanthropic efforts. Organizations like the Bill and Melinda Gates Foundation have made significant investments in global health initiatives, such as vaccine development, infectious disease control, and maternal and child health. These efforts have contributed to substantial progress in reducing disease burden and improving health outcomes in low- and middle-income countries.

While philanthropy has made significant contributions to healthcare, there are challenges to consider. Ensuring the sustainability of healthcare initiatives, addressing health disparities, and promoting equity are critical considerations for philanthropists. Collaboration with healthcare providers, policymakers, and communities is essential to create lasting impact and improve health outcomes for all.

13

Chapter 13: Philanthropy and the Arts

The arts have long been a beneficiary of philanthropic support, with wealthy individuals and foundations recognizing the value of the arts in enriching lives, fostering creativity, and promoting cultural understanding. Philanthropy in the arts encompasses a wide range of activities, from funding museums and performing arts organizations to supporting individual artists and arts education programs.

One prominent example of philanthropic support in the arts is the work of the Andrew W. Mellon Foundation. The foundation supports a diverse array of arts and cultural organizations, including museums, theaters, and music institutions. The Mellon Foundation's grants focus on areas such as arts education, conservation, and public access to the arts. By supporting the arts, the foundation aims to promote creativity, preserve cultural heritage, and ensure that the arts are accessible to all.

Another example is the work of the Getty Foundation, which supports visual arts and cultural heritage initiatives around the world. The foundation funds projects in areas such as art conservation, research, and education. The Getty Foundation's grants help preserve and protect important works of art and cultural heritage, ensuring that future generations can appreciate and learn from them.

Philanthropy in the arts also includes support for individual artists and arts education programs. Organizations like the MacArthur Foundation provide fellowships and grants to artists, writers, and performers, enabling them to pursue their creative work. Arts education programs, such as those supported by the Wallace Foundation, aim to provide access to high-quality arts education for students of all backgrounds. These programs help nurture creativity, critical thinking, and cultural understanding in young people.

While philanthropy has made significant contributions to the arts, there are challenges to consider. Ensuring equity and diversity in arts funding, addressing the needs of underserved communities, and promoting sustainability are critical considerations for philanthropists. Collaboration with arts organizations, educators, and communities is essential to create lasting impact and ensure that the arts continue to thrive.

14

Chapter 14: The Future of Philanthropy

As we look to the future, philanthropy is likely to continue evolving in response to emerging challenges and opportunities. Several key trends and developments are shaping the future of philanthropy, including the rise of digital technology, the growing focus on social justice, and the increasing importance of collaboration.

Digital technology is expected to play an even more significant role in the future of philanthropy. Advances in data analytics, artificial intelligence, and blockchain technology have the potential to enhance the effectiveness and transparency of philanthropic efforts. These technologies can help philanthropists make more informed decisions, track the impact of their contributions, and ensure that resources are used efficiently.

The growing focus on social justice is also likely to shape the future of philanthropy. As awareness of systemic inequality and social injustice increases, philanthropists are placing greater emphasis on initiatives that promote equity, inclusion, and systemic change. This shift towards social justice philanthropy involves addressing the root causes of inequality and ensuring that the voices of marginalized communities are centered in philanthropic efforts.

Collaboration is another key trend in the future of philanthropy. The complexity of global challenges requires collective action and multi-stakeholder partnerships. Philanthropists are increasingly working together, as well as with governments, businesses, and civil society organizations, to maximize their impact and drive systemic change. Collaborative initiatives can leverage the strengths and expertise of multiple stakeholders, creating more effective and sustainable solutions.

In addition to these trends, the future of philanthropy will also be shaped by the evolving values and priorities of the next generation of philanthropists. Younger philanthropists are often driven by a strong sense of social responsibility and a desire to create meaningful change. They are more likely to embrace innovative approaches, take risks, and prioritize impact over tradition.

As philanthropy continues to evolve, it will be essential for philanthropists to remain flexible, responsive, and attuned to the changing needs of society. By embracing new technologies, promoting social justice, and fostering collaboration, philanthropists can create a more inclusive and impactful future.

15

Chapter 15: The Intersection of Philanthropy and Politics

Philanthropy and politics have long been intertwined, as wealthy individuals and foundations use their resources to influence public policy and drive social change. Political philanthropy can take various forms, including funding advocacy campaigns, supporting policy research, and engaging in direct political activities. While political philanthropy has the potential to create significant impact, it also raises important ethical and governance questions.

One prominent example of political philanthropy is the work of the Open Society Foundations, founded by billionaire financier George Soros. The foundation supports initiatives that promote democracy, human rights, and social justice around the world. Through funding for civil society organizations, advocacy campaigns, and policy research, the Open Society Foundations aim to address systemic issues and promote open and inclusive societies. Soros' political philanthropy has sparked both admiration and controversy, highlighting the complex dynamics of using private wealth to influence public policy.

Another example is the work of the Koch brothers, Charles and David Koch, who have used their wealth to support libertarian and conservative causes. Through their network of foundations, think tanks, and advocacy organizations, the Koch brothers have funded efforts to promote free-market policies, reduce government regulation, and influence electoral outcomes. Their political philanthropy has had a significant impact on American politics, shaping policy debates and mobilizing grassroots support for their causes.

Political philanthropy is not limited to the United States. Globally, wealthy individuals and foundations are using their resources to influence political processes and advocate for social change. For instance, philanthropists in Europe and Latin America have funded initiatives to promote democratic governance, human rights, and social justice. These efforts often involve collaboration with civil society organizations, think tanks, and advocacy groups to amplify their impact.

While political philanthropy can drive meaningful change, it also raises ethical and governance questions. Critics argue that the influence of wealthy donors in politics can undermine democratic processes and create power imbalances. There are concerns about transparency and accountability, as political philanthropy can sometimes operate outside the public eye. To address these challenges, it is essential for political philanthropists to engage in ethical practices, ensure transparency, and prioritize the voices and needs of the communities they seek to support.

16

Chapter 16: Philanthropy in Times of Crisis

In times of crisis, philanthropy plays a critical role in providing immediate relief and supporting long-term recovery efforts. Wealthy individuals, foundations, and corporations mobilize resources to address urgent needs and help communities rebuild and recover. Crisis philanthropy encompasses a wide range of activities, from disaster relief and humanitarian aid to supporting social services and economic recovery.

One prominent example of crisis philanthropy is the response to the COVID-19 pandemic. Philanthropists around the world mobilized resources to support healthcare systems, provide economic relief, and address the social and economic impacts of the pandemic. The Gates Foundation, for instance, committed significant funding to support vaccine development, diagnostics, and treatments for COVID-19. The foundation also worked to ensure that vaccines and treatments were accessible to low- and middle-income countries.

Another example is the response to natural disasters, such as hurricanes, earthquakes, and wildfires. Philanthropists often provide immediate relief through donations to humanitarian organizations, such as the Red Cross and UNICEF. These contributions support emergency response efforts, including food, shelter, and medical care for affected communities. In addition to immediate relief, philanthropists also invest in long-term recovery and resilience efforts, such as rebuilding infrastructure, supporting mental health services, and promoting disaster preparedness.

Crisis philanthropy is not limited to natural disasters and public health emergencies. Philanthropists also respond to social and economic crises, such as poverty, homelessness, and social unrest. For example, during the economic recession of 2008, philanthropists provided funding to support social services, job training programs, and economic development initiatives. Similarly, in response to social movements for racial justice, philanthropists have supported initiatives that address systemic racism, promote equity, and support communities of color.

While crisis philanthropy is essential in times of need, it also presents challenges. Ensuring the effective and equitable distribution of resources, coordinating with other stakeholders, and addressing long-term needs are critical considerations for philanthropists. Collaboration with governments, humanitarian organizations, and affected communities is essential to maximize the impact of crisis philanthropy and support sustainable recovery.

17

Chapter 17: The Legacy of Philanthropy

The legacy of philanthropy is shaped by the enduring impact of charitable efforts and the values and principles that guide giving. Wealthy individuals and foundations often seek to create a lasting legacy through their philanthropic contributions, whether by addressing specific social issues, supporting communities, or promoting systemic change.

One notable example of a lasting philanthropic legacy is the work of Andrew Carnegie, whose contributions to education and libraries continue to benefit communities today. Carnegie's philosophy of the "Gospel of Wealth" emphasized the responsibility of the wealthy to use their resources for the public good. His legacy is evident in the thousands of libraries he funded, as well as the institutions he established, such as Carnegie Mellon University and the Carnegie Foundation for the Advancement of Teaching.

Another example is the legacy of the Rockefeller Foundation, which has made significant contributions to public health, scientific research, and social progress. The foundation's funding for medical research has led to groundbreaking discoveries and advancements in healthcare. Its support for education and social justice initiatives has had a lasting impact on communities around the world. The Rockefeller Foundation's legacy is characterized by its long-term commitment to addressing complex social issues and promoting positive change.

Philanthropists also create lasting legacies through endowed funds and foundations that continue to support charitable initiatives after their lifetimes. Endowed funds provide a sustainable source of funding for specific causes, ensuring that philanthropic efforts can continue for generations to come. Foundations often establish programs and initiatives that address evolving social challenges and adapt to changing needs.

The legacy of philanthropy is not limited to individual contributions. Collaborative efforts and partnerships also leave a lasting impact on society. Initiatives like The Giving Pledge, which encourages billionaires to commit the majority of their wealth to philanthropy, have inspired a new generation of philanthropists and created a culture of giving. Collaborative efforts that address global challenges, such as climate change and public health, have the potential to create systemic and enduring change.

As we reflect on the legacy of philanthropy, it is important to consider the values and principles that guide giving. Ethical considerations, transparency, accountability, and a focus on equity and inclusion are essential to creating a positive and lasting legacy. By embracing these principles, philanthropists can ensure that their contributions make a meaningful and lasting impact on society.

In **"Philanthropy Unbound: How the Wealthy Rewrite the Rules of Giving,"** journey through the transformative world of modern philanthropy, where the affluent leverage their vast resources to reshape the landscape of charitable giving. This compelling narrative delves into the history, strategies, and ethical dilemmas faced by today's most influential philanthropists.

From the early efforts of pioneers like Andrew Carnegie and John D. Rockefeller to the innovative approaches of tech titans such as Bill Gates and Mark Zuckerberg, this book explores how the wealthy have continually redefined what it means to give. It examines the rise of global philanthropy, the power of collaboration, and the role of technology in amplifying impact.

Readers will uncover the complexities of social justice philanthropy, the influence of corporate giving, and the critical role of family foundations. Each chapter sheds light on the challenges and opportunities that come with wielding immense philanthropic power, offering insights into the motivations and aspirations of those who seek to create lasting change.

CHAPTER 17: THE LEGACY OF PHILANTHROPY

"Philanthropy Unbound" also addresses the ethical considerations and potential pitfalls of modern philanthropy, urging a thoughtful and responsible approach to giving. By providing a comprehensive overview of the current philanthropic landscape, this book invites readers to reflect on the evolving nature of generosity and its profound impact on society.

Perfect for anyone interested in the intersection of wealth, power, and social good, "Philanthropy Unbound: How the Wealthy Rewrite the Rules of Giving" is a thought-provoking and enlightening read that reveals the true power and potential of philanthropy in our world today.

www.ingramcontent.com/pod-product-compliance
Lightning Source LLC
LaVergne TN
LVHW020458080526
838202LV00057B/6020